Smoke Rising

Also by John Seed

Poetry
Spaces In (Pig Press, Newcastle-upon Tyne 1977)
History Labour Night (Pig Press, Durham 1984)
Interior in the Open Air (Reality Studios, London 1993)
Divided into One (Poetical Histories, Cambridge 2003)
New and Collected Poems (Shearsman Books, Exeter 2005)
Pictures from Mayhew (Shearsman Books, Exeter 2005)
That Barrikins (Shearsman Books, Exeter 2007)
Manchester: August 16th & 17th 1819 (Intercapillary Editions, London 2013)
Some Poems, 2006-12 (Gratton Street Irregulars, Cheltenham, 2014)

Other Books
The Culture of Capital. Art, power and the nineteenth-century middle class [co-edited with Janet Wolff]
    (Manchester: Manchester University Press 1988, paperback 1990)
Cultural Revolution. The Challenge of the Arts in the 1960s [co-edited with Bart Moore-Gilbert]
    (London: Routledge, 1992)
Dissenting Histories: religious division and the politics of memory in eighteenth-century England
    (Edinburgh: Edinburgh University Press, 2008)
Marx: A Guide for the Perplexed (London: Continuum, paperback, 2010)
The Gordon Riots [coedited with Ian Haywood] (Cambridge: Cambridge University Press, 2012, 2014).

John Seed

Smoke Rising

London 1940-1

Shearsman Books

First published in the United Kingdom in 2015 by
Shearsman Books
50 Westons Hill Drive
Emersons Green
BRISTOL
BS16 7DF

Shearsman Books Ltd Registered Office
30–31 St. James Place, Mangotsfield, Bristol BS16 9JB
(this address not for correspondence)

www.shearsman.com

ISBN 978-1-84861-432-1

ACKNOWLEDGEMENTS
Five sections have appeared in *Shadowtrain* 20 (Nov/Dec.2007),
http://www.shadowtrain.com/id210.html

Nebuchadnez'zar spake and said unto them, Is it true, O Shadrach, Meshach, and Abed'nego? do not ye serve my gods, nor worship the golden image which I have set up?

Now if ye be ready that at what time ye hear the sound of the cornet, flute, harp, sackbut, psaltery, and dulcimer, and all kinds of music, ye fall down and worship the image which I have made; well: but if ye worship not, ye shall be cast the same hour into the midst of a burning fiery furnace; and who is that God that shall deliver you out of my hands?

Shadrach, Meshach, and Abed'nego, answered and said to the king, O Nebuchadnez'zar, we are not careful to answer thee in this matter.

If it be so, our God whom we serve is able to deliver us from the burning fiery furnace, and he will deliver us out of thine hand, O king.

But if not, be it known unto thee, O king, that we will not serve thy gods, nor worship the golden image which thou hast set up.

Book of Daniel, 3: 14-18

Wind a maximum 12 miles per hour
8/10ths cloud earlier on but clearing fast
forecasters predict calm and fine with slight mists

12,000 feet
flying a steady 180 m.p.h.
the French coast in forty minutes
another eighteen minutes to the English coast
then sixteen minutes to London

radio guide beams
southwest-to-northeast axis
intersecting
main "X" beam over West Ham
a steady regular pulsing
in each wireless operator's ears

from other stations along the French coast
decoy beams crisscrossing
other sectors of the capital

———————

Best nights
moonlit

nights
after rain

shadows of
buildings and

moonlight
reflect from

wet streets
and squares

London
below

clear and readable
as a map

_____

The bomber will always get through

Wherever an object can be seen from the air

man in the street there is no

power on earth

_____

Room logged the
crash found even
Deptford Warden
Albert at Fighter
Command the
engines never ceased
were left frequency
other bomber gone
bombers in bright

but how every radar
station reported
bombers every fifteen
minutes a No. 1 Raid
meant a wave that at
12.45 a.m. nobody
knew too high for
visual checks even
moonlight

ten plus planes
tonight was a wave
and the planes flew
centres used gallows
whining cadence of
midnight had fallen
down the high-
pitched noise of
minutes

_____

tonight's siren after black-out

hearts once more tighten and sink you
keep that date with fear
sleepless into the small hours"

——————

Summer evenings watching the sun
after the long weekend
setting on a bedroom wall might be
gone before dawn

——————

Almost any room will serve as a refuge-room if it
is soundly constructed and smoke if it is easy
to reach and to get out of don't light fires
so that no light is visible from outside smother them
with earth or sand preferably facing a building or blank
wall or a narrow street or salt listening to the
wireless or gramophone take care when coming out of your
refuge-room sit or preferably lie down and keep still
fires cause currents of air which may draw in gas don't

from outside skylights fanlights glazed doors a tempest dropping fire
so that no light is visible from outside extinguish all
fires in grates don't let the children romp about unless
the room is damaged don't smoke unless you have to
go out do not put out these fires where lights
are used with water must be completely screened after dusk
unless keeping warm with blankets you actually smell gas don't
until you hear the "Raiders Passed" signal a continuous signal
lasting two minutes don't go out at a steady pitch

───────────

Countering the Air Raid Menace the Protection of Home

Where two children were killed this was the nursery with toys around the bed

The redhill sand container the stirrup water pump

Long-handled shovel and rake for fighting incendiary bombs

There has been a great demand in London for deck chairs and camp beds

Coat all woodwork in the roof space with lime-wash apply two coats

See that flues are sealed against gas

It took one ton of bombs to kill three-quarters of a person

Brick partition walls are better than lath and plaster

Do not put on your respirator unless

Sand bags in front of the refuge room sealed windows floor and flue its door hung with a wet

protecting blanket

'I used to live in London but London is all bombed and gone and all the houses have fallen down'.

———————

I've just discovered
we've been getting the sirens mixed

> darting in at the continuous blast
>
> coming out again at the warbling note

———————

IF YOU THROW A BUCKET OF WATER ON A BURNING INCENDIARY BOMB IT
WILL EXPLODE AND THROW BURNING FRAGMENTS IN ALL DIRECTIONS.

So stand it up by a brick wall

Lay on it

Leave it to a Warden

Flop a coat over it or throw it into a sewer or anywhere there is water

Pick it up and run it in water

Sit back and hold tight

Leave it where it is and run

Keep the thin places of your house patched up

Put on your gas-mask

———————

You can tell how many
people live in every house
by the number of packed
suitcases in the hall ready

———————

on foot from the next night's terror
five thousand trudge out nightly into Epping
Forest they sleep in the open air

——————

13/6/40 Evacuees leaving Paddington

children jostling
shepherded in sheds
luggage labels round their necks
clutching gas-masks
little suitcases boxes brown-paper bags

a very small boy dragging a big kit bag
little girl a doll close to her face

Policeman asked a little girl: "Where do you think you're going?"
Small boy about 5 answered: "Going to win the war mate."

Young ones full of fun
older ones kept silent
looked at the soldiers
and seemed to realise
what their departure meant

to the grown-ups who

who looked on

—————

A railway station

doors closed

and a few people outside

reading books and papers

occasionally glance skywards

—————

"It is the policy of London Transport that omnibuses should continue to run unless an attack seems likely in the immediate vicinity, in which event the driver must pull up at a shelter, stop near the curb, or turn into a side street."

[*The Times*, 28 Aug 1940]

—————

revolving door painted black spinning you out into the dark the rain had stopped

clatter of footsteps echoes and clanks a bus changing gear

put out your hands

white gloves and you feel sandbags and then nothing

at the crossroads no signposts invisible in the dark names painted out

little bright X's mark obstructions in the road a hooded lamp-post's thin beam

shine a torch on your hands your

white gloves

—————

Raids day & night

Dreadful things were happening we could hear under the stairs in the cellar we sleep in fits and starts continual droning from many planes overhead distant bomb explosions some of them very loud heard a bomb come hurtling down it sounded so close we thought it must be coming on us it struck the ground the house shook violently sound of breaking glass falling bricks

—————

Walking towards Mile end road   blankets and rugs under their arms:

They say the whole of Smithy Street will be evacuated
shouldn't be surprised
terribly old houses
and every time a bomb drops anywhere near the plaster falls in

I don't suppose we'll ever see Smithy street again it was
queer coming back

we've only been away two days but
we expected to see it
done in

———————

One moment the street was dark the next illuminated by a
hundred sizzling
bluish-white flames curious
plop-plopping sound as they fell they seemed to
sprout
not
drop from the skies

———————

19.9.40 Stepney

Evacuation you know what they did?

sent us to Kennington   and when we got there we found the place crawling with insects   and dirty?

we could scoop it up in our hands   we said we couldn't stay there so they're finding us another billet

but meanwhile we have come home   absolutely at their mercy that's the annoying part they can

dilly-dally for days

———————

we've been over to Dempsey Street school as many as three times a day but it's no good

either they can't be bothered or else they're too full already

I think they've got a lot on their hands

we're not the only ones but

of course we think of ourselves first

I wish I could have saved an overcoat or something

I've had to borrow money for a new one we've

got to have clothes

———————

I don't think they'll do

anything for you

until you're dead

and even then there's

no money for a funeral

_____

Fires were raging again this morn'g & smoke & burnt powder fills the air.

A very little rain fell in the night.

3 sirens again today but we kept busy downstairs & made my bread.

Lovely rain now falling

but our roof slates are

not on yet.

_____

Smithy Street, 14.9.40

Mrs Kalinsky: Let's stay here and chance it tonight eh?

Mr Kalinsky: Stay here and chance it then. If *you* stay here, *I* stay here. If *you* go up west, *I* go up West. – What's the difference?

_____

> burning rags and paper
> raining down
> on High Street
> walking dodging flaming stuff
> a tempest dropping fire

> leaving Stepney
> in a rain of ash

All that first week of the Blitz there had been so much smoke and dust we couldn't see the sky and when we got to Ealing we saw clear blue skies and it was a shock to realize it was still summer.

———————

14.9.40

Streets are moving out wholesale. Notes pinned to front doors (Dempsey Street):

> GONE TO HOTEL HENDERSON SEE YOU THERE
> HAD TO CLEAR OUT BOMB AT BACK
> CANCEL NEWSPAPER ORDER GONE TO COUNTRY
> UP WEST END SHANT BE BACK THIS WEEK

———————

All Clear this morn'g went at 5. am & we thankfully undressed & got between the sheets & Ethel went up to her own bed.

Just settling off to sleep when Siren again & followed by a heavy explosion which as Ethel says shot her out of bed in no time & she came back to her fix up downstairs, 1/2 an hour later All Clear so we had an hour's sleep.

———————

Watching from the roof formations of
planes more than I ever saw
in one sky before
criss-crossing
Alice-blue snow-white smoke trails

———————

Trafalgar Square the fountains dry
Eros a mound of sandbags

Twilit alleys behind the cinemas
Ladies of the evening
Silver-fox capes pocket torches
Patrolled before the shopkeeper's signs
Business as Usual

———————

end wall of the nurses' home
Cheyne Hospital for Children
undamaged to about two-thirds up

the second floor where the brickwork had been
sucked away along a clean line from back to front
leaving the top floor exposed in section

floor joists to roof space
made-up bed a chair an open wardrobe
ceiling light still burning

––––––––––

Monday 9 September a beautiful summer night so warm
red glow from the East the docks burning

out in the open we stared for a minute
and I tried to fix the scene in my mind

because one day this will be history

and I
shall be one of those who actually saw it I wasn't

frightened any more the searchlights
were beautiful it was like

like watching the end of the world

Racing towards the house feeling the air all around as if the whole air was falling apart

silently then suddenly I was on my face inside the kitchen door there seemed to be waves buffeting me
one after another like bathing in a rough sea I remember clutching at the floor the carpet was a cliff-
face I had to hang on to prevent myself being swept away

———————

dry scratching rattle shrapnel roof

thud of walls collapsing

sharp taps incendiaries

The British Museum opposite my window
rose-red in the light of the fire of the University. Every now and then it turns sharp white when a
magnesium flare descends. Then rose-red again

'Thank God Jack's safe in the army'

———————

about twenty past one in the morning
I was reading *The Taming of the Shrew* in bed the
windows blew in the room
was filled with a greenish dust
all the furniture
moved
not far it all
moved
about a foot

———————

Slept for an hour
& missed
hearing the
All Clear.

———————

Alexandra Hotel in the main lounge a marble pillar snapped like a tree trunk toppled with a crack walls
burst apart raining light brackets mirrors clocks chunks of ceiling the
ground floor split open debris
thundered to the basement

steel emergency stairs running down the outside wall

warped and twisted

climbed to the sky

                        bedrooms open to the moonlit park

———————

a screaming sound   threw ourselves to the bedroom floor there was

a shattering explosion followed

by what sounded like tin cans falling incendiaries

———————

Bright moonlight of Saturday-night London

Oh Johnny the band was playing

outside guns crashed

an explosion somewhere above

interrupts the speaker in mid-word

and the ceiling fell in and the lights went out

filled with dust and fumes blackened faces and frocks dancers searching with torches for their partners

a few seconds before

first impression somebody had thrown a bottle in my face from the balcony I saw this blue flash and everything in the air I stood with a glass in my hand chatting then a sudden very severe pressure on the top of my head then complete darkness opening my eyes the Cafe de Paris was in semi-darkness groans low cries whimpering sitting on the floor back against the wall a man was leaning over me a glass in his hand he told me to drink it was *sal volatile* when I sort of came to I was sitting on somebody an officer wearing a kilt I discovered my leg was broken and my back was very wet a lot of dust bodies lying around lights burning darkness

_____

Family having supper in the kitchen tremendous uproar from the scullery great

crashings

of slates falling they tried to get in pushing against the scullery door

was jammed so they went out of the front round to the back

and found a land-mine
covered in soot
propped against the scullery door

_____

for Tony Frazer

it's supposed to buzz for fifteen seconds and then go off

but some of them buzz a few seconds and go off

the important thing when dealing with these mines
if you have to move them at all
before you take the fuse out

listen

very carefully

all the time

and if you hear it start to buzz run like hell because you might have up to fifteen seconds

———————

Illustrated London News

A family whose home was demolished in a raid on August 15th cheerfully survey the belongings they managed to salvage

A woman who had a miraculous escape with four children when sheltering beneath a staircase retrieves a money-box

An Anderson shelter correctly covered with earth from which cabbages sprout

A nurse at the Great Ormond Street Hospital for Sick Children displays the percussion cap and winged tail of a bomb

A school a classroom with desks overturned and burned rafters

Glare of the fire in the docks and other scattered outbreaks reflected upon clouds and smoke united to form one huge glow giving a grim impression of miles and miles of London on fire   actually the fires were circumscribed and strictly local in character

Desecration of the Mecca of the Victorian bucks a bomb in the Burlington Arcade

In the first drawing a doctor is seen making his round of shattered houses where people are being dug out of the ruins a limb having been uncovered by the rescue squad the doctor feels the pulse and if there is any sign of life he makes an injection

Bombed twice on successive nights the crater in the wreckage marks the spot where the second bomb fell beside the first

Corner of a ward in a London hospital nurses removing bedclothes from under fallen beams

Ear-plugs for all the ear-drums of the public are to be protected by a Government free issue of ear-plugs above several million pairs are shortly to be issued

Anti-blast adhesive netting rendering omnibus windows blast-proof

Bomb falling in water

———————

swimming pool built for the princesses in what was a conservatory at the NW corner of the palace suffered a direct hit the diving stand lies twisted side-ways sharing London's lot their majesties view their damaged home by a block of LCC flats in South London showing their majesties bomb crater the nature of Goering's work these tenants of a block of flats had their raider's end shot to pieces over Victoria outside the big gun crashed again and the glasses shook

homes bombed as their majesties' own home had been not a pane of glass was left intact in the North front where both the king and queen's apartments are the bomb landed near the queen's sitting-room on the first floor the Chinese Chippendale room bricks fell into the picture gallery stone pillars two-feet in diameter were broken into pieces a Buckingham Palace on the table the king and queen were not in residence and no one in the palace was hurt

———————

it'll hit you

if yer number's on it

St. Pancras Station
parachute hanging from a signal
lying on the track between Platforms One and Two

black eight-foot cylinder
white lettering
1991

————————

Exmouth Street it's terrible
legs and arms of
little children all burned
and scarred you can
see them through the
bricks little children no
more the Simons such
nice people they was

————————

Searchlights moving in awkward arcs crossing and re-crossing   column of dust 200 feet into the air
the explosion of a bomb is usually called a bang   the angle is almost vertical and when they hit the
roof they drop through the building and explode in the basement   between rows of houses a gap
where a house was   into the midst of a burning fiery furnace   mass of bricks and rubble and brick-
dust in which she was buried a tattered cinema poster "So Ends Our Night"

————————

An empty Baptist church was hit the roof blown off

a man posting letters some distance away was killed by the blast

the premises to which these letters were addressed
was razed to the ground

half a ton of bombs to kill three-eighths of a person

one bomb fell on the premises of an undertaker
demolished the building
and killed the undertaker his wife their son daughter-in-law and grandchild

———————

Moorgate Station burned out

heat so intense glass and aluminium melted to form pools

gas mains white pillars 50 feet high burning
idle pumps coils of empty hose

a land-mine dropped almost at the centre of a cross-roads
four houses on the four corners five stories high were obliterated

patient after patient

M on foreheads scrawled in skin pencil   "morphia needed"

———————

"The violent and indiscriminate bombing of London during the past two or three days has naturally caused some temporary dislocation of travelling facilities. In order to enable the work of restoring the services to proceed with the least possible delay the public are asked to refrain from unnecessary travel to and from the London area."

[Ministry of Transport: 11 September 1940]

———————

Blasted windows clocks without hands glass

on stairs mounds of yellow

rubble poisonous tang of damp plaster

and coal gas the house still

smouldering scraps of cloth hanging bare

walls at the side still standing

burnt piece of wood like a

gibbet jutted out into the sky

weary blistered firemen grimy half-clad

homeless mirror swinging steeples scorched and

discoloured by fire the sound of

swept off the streets a few

seconds above the trees lines of

figures asleep scrawled over

obscene inscriptions

————————

usual two daytime raids

one siren before 9

our day's work

began in shelters we all

trooped down to the safe

a communal effort *The Times Crossword*

and later idle chatter

some read one or two doze

a few smoke

but most of us chatter

————————

And every evening about five he goes home to his ruins

gardening between thunderstorms and air raids

raking shrapnel from the lawn

———————

The noise of the siren is getting more people down than anything else the scream of these unspeakable instruments after six hours sleep last night really made me quite ill

the extreme melancholy of the present "woman-wailing-for-her-demon-lover" warning seems to constitute a serious strain on the toughest morale

could we not make use of the inspiriting air of 'The Campbells are coming' conveying a definite warning   at the same time it implies a hearty defiance and a certain zest for the fray

for the all-clear we could hardly do better than 'Who's afraid of the big bad wolf'

———————

Up the long escalator
six storeys high people

sitting both sides
families children arms around

each other stretched along
the railings sleeping

underground city of people
in their first sleep

_____

East-End shelters sole illumination a hurricane lantern the visitor picks his steps among human bodies huddled on mud floors fearful of treading on a human face

Every time there is a bomb a burst of hysterical singing from the next shelter 25 yards away shut your bleedin' row we've got enough noise without you

a tremendous crash wakes everybody up drawn breath waiting for more stop leaning on the wall you bloody fool all we do is eat sleep and go to the shelters

_____

24.9.40

His wife and children have been evacuated they went yesterday
in a bus we don't know where they're going they were taken to Notting Hill that's not very far but
they're supposed to go somewhere else from there
She's glad to get out of it
Why don't *you* go?

I can't leave my work

Where do you sleep?

    In the West End I work there so I sleep in the shelter and go straight to my work I've got no home

—————

dim figures in dejected heaps on unwashed floors in total darkness

each September night the floor crowded with some two or three hundred homeless people lying on blankets mattresses and piles of clothing

ten pails and coal-scuttles to use as lavatories by the middle of the night overflowing as the night advances urine and faeces spread in ever-increasing volume over the floor the space is narrow whoever enters inevitably steps in the sewage and carries it on his shoes all over the building by dawn the stench   there were seven basins to wash in but no soap or towels.

—————

out of the noises came music a guitar I smelled cigarette smoke a single dim blue light.

This is the social end American jazz with cockney accents.

"We call that end of the shelter the Ritz."

—————

I can't
stand it

it's
killing me

this ain't war
this is murder it's
absolutely killing me
I'm going
to stay with my sister in Tottenham

_____

"Is it possible to make a rule that all people who snore or have colds should sleep in a walled-off portion of London air-raid shelters? Bombs and gunfire noises are bearable compared with continuous snoring."

_____

We've got a kind of
        system when there's a hit
everybody comes out and we
        get together and go from
one shelter to another to

see if everybody is alright
to be sure the entrance
        hasn't caved in and they
can't get out then we
        go back into our holes

––––––––––––

harassed bustling determinedly cheerful helpers
corned beef sandwiches and tea the
London County Council panacea for hunger shock
loss misery and illness dishevelled
half-dressed people wandering between bombed
houses and the rest centre
salvaging bits and pieces a
clergyman appeared and wandered about
aimlessly someone played the piano

––––––––––

Tilbury shelter part of the
Liverpool Street goods
station off Commercial Road
Stepney people queued from
midday waiting for the gates
to open at four-thirty service
men on leave kept places for
their families at work
unevacuated school-children
were proxies for relatives
men and women every age
oblivious of daylight sirens
and dog-fights overhead if
they took shelter they lost
their places in the queue and
their option on their favourite
sleeping-spot for the night
when the gates opened the
police linked hands to stem
the rush down the slope on a
wet night there were over
14,000 people seamen came
in for a few hours between
tides prostitutes paraded
hawkers sold fried fish the
police broke up fights
children slept

———————

Is the water all right ducks do you
think it'll be all right do you think
we'll be able to get our dinner in
the oven in time before the gas goes

off again I don't know every time I
start to get me dinner in the oven
so the blessed warning goes off goes the
gas again into the shelter again and then

we come back again and there's the dinner
all spoilt and if you forget to turn

the gas off well your dinner was absolutely
done for and bang's gone your rations again

———————

          Clouds of black smoke an old man
          repeating they'll never get home

          no not one of them they'll
          all go down

          those that do things like that
          never get home no
          never they'll

———————

And then we got safely in the shelter again
and everything was all quiet that night we was all right
and the children asleep all right
and then just as we were coming out in the morning
up goes Moaning Minnie
back in the shelter you'd go again
and the women'd say
oh bless me what time we going to get to work this morning?

Well we get to work and you're absolutely tired
and as soon as you get to work up goes the warning again
down goes the bucket and pails into the shelter you're downstairs again

upstairs you come again
and then the boss'd say how much work you done
then when you turn round and tell him you've been up all night he says
poor old souls but still never mind I suppose it's the Lord's wish that we've got to carry on like this but still
it won't be for ever
and we used to say no

but if it was for any longer
we wouldn't put up with it

———————

Anderson shelter where a bomb
dropped was afire and two

women and two kiddies was in
this here shelter in a very

very short time we had the
emergency door down and these people

out of the shelter and today
I see them walking up and

down the road but every time
my missus opens the oven I

think about that shelter a little
while longer and they'd have come

out like a rabbit comes out
of your stove on a Sunday

———————

In one of my shelters unbeknown to us they moved in a piano

first I heard of it they'd all come out of the pub it was a proper bedlam it was like Barley Fair they was
singing and dancing

and they said you'd better come over Doll because you know the people and you can deal with 'em

well I will say this I grew up with some of these people and rough as they was they didn't make it too hard because people did want their rest and up to a certain time yes you're allowed a singsong like you was in an ordinary house but when you went into the early morning it had to be stopped and let other people get their rest because if you got a bad night in the shelter you didn't feel as if you could work next day

oh I might tell you we had some lively times mouth organs in one the piano in the other a plague of mosquitoes that winter refusing to hibernate winds howled through the tunnels the stench of human excrement the Church used to hold a service but the kiddies used to come in there eating potatoes and hot dogs running around fetching their homework making stools for the shelter so that fell off

—————

My heart misses a beat
interrupts a speaker in mid-word
whenever a car changes gear
when someone runs or walks very quickly or suddenly stands still or cocks their head on one side or stares up at the sky or says "Sssshhh!"

or whistles blow or a door bangs in the wind or a mosquito buzzes in the room or

Noticed a good many amulets and crosses and charms being worn lately

                    Lay in the shelter most of night
                    face down pillow over my head

—————

Shelter in comfort   Warm Raid Wear

Step-in Raid Suit of soft wool with zip front cosy hood tie belt and two good pockets

Three-quarter wool Raid Coat heavier weight llama finished wool with broad shoulders and good wrap

very warm and light in navy purple rose three shades of blue warm brown and green

Serviceable Raid Suit in heavy water-proofed wool with cosy hood lined lamb's wool torch pocket and

two trouser pockets in Air-force blue nigger golden brown navy and black

———————

this time bomb at the back of the garden

and the wardens came round and said

we'd have to evacuate the house

take shelter elsewhere

so

they put us underneath the railway arch

———————

The occasion instant decision difficult fragments

of speech hallucinations philosophical

propositions anecdotes quarterly reports winter

of bereavements administration of the dead is a

change of address

bells of the fire service clanging

east along the high road

we're in the front line

me own home
it's in the Front Line

———————

24.9.40

After all he's a warden
so he should get better treatment

It ain't fair taking him to Redman's Road
there ain't no proper people there as can see to it

There he was
couldn't hardly move for the pain of it
and they just left him lying on the floor
no proper bed nor anything

———————

Dorchester Hotel
Turkish baths air-raid shelter

Neat row of cots two feet apart
Each one covered with a fluffy eiderdown

Pillows large and full and white
Silks billowed and shone
In the dim light in
Pale pinks and blues

Behind each cot hung
The negligée the dressing-gown

A little sign
Pinned to one of the curtains
Reserved for Lord Halifax Lord
Fucking Halifax

———————

Blackout on carriage windows a new scribbling pad.
"Blinds must be kept down after dark" is varied to "Blonds must be kept down after dark" and to
"Knickers must be kept down after dark."
Many pencil scribbles of no meaning at all, lines and dots and circles.

———————

By 4.00 p.m. all the platforms and passages of the underground station are staked out, chiefly
with blankets folded in long strips laid against the wall – the trains are still running and the

platforms in use. A woman or child guards places for about six people.
Until the evening comes

and the rest of the family crowd in

> lines of corpse-like figures
> asleep among their household goods
> until the morning siren

Some slept in a sitting position
backs to the tunnel walls

———————

Oval station a narrow path
bordered on either side by people lying prone
men women boys girls babies three deep on either side
on mattresses and blankets
spread out on the floor

———————

to keep part of the platforms clear for travellers officials painted two white lines
one eight feet and the other four feet from the platform's edge
until half past seven shelterers were not supposed to cross the eight-foot line
after the rush hour until half past ten four feet of platform were kept clear for travellers

at about nine the adults began to settle down for the night

it rapidly became impossible to move about because of the sprawling bodies

one policeman and one shelter marshal on duty

tried to keep a passageway clear

but once the people were lying down they more or less gave up

half past ten the train service was discontinued

lights dimmed at the request of the shelterers but not extinguished

current cut off in the electric rail

—————

Last night I was down the tube at Piccadilly I've never been there before

my it was a scream I hadn't got anything you see no blankets anything

and there was an old man next to me a dear old man he was (laughs)

and he said would I like to share his bag so I said yes (laughs)

and we lay there like that it was a scream didn't he snore too it was a scream and in the morning he

said to me how did you enjoy sharing my virtuous bed

you do feel safe you know nothing can get you there and that's a marvellous feeling

after these nights

            I know some people say if it's coming for you it's coming

      fate kind of thing

but I don't believe in that if you believe in that you can go out enjoy yourself do what you like but I

don't believe in it
I wouldn't go out in them

―――――――

In a Westminster Hospital
bed an LCC clerk of works
whose duty was to identify
and tabulate unexploded

bombs wounded twice on the
same day two bombs burst
near his car after his wounds
were dressed at an emergency

hospital in the street again a
land-mine exploded
showering him in broken
glass

―――――――

somehow I don't worry about it

if you let yourself think what might drop on you
you get all scared like

better sleep and not think

that's my recipe

―――――――

The train's windows covered with opaque or black-out material
stopped at a station the doors open

      platform crowded from end to end
      five deep thousands of them
      on mattresses surrounded by blankets pillows suitcases
      raised on one arm or sitting up eating sandwiches chocolate or fruit
      drinking beer or tea out of thermos flasks
      others talking and reading or playing cards
      others marching up and down a narrow pathway
      two feet wide at the edge of the platform it was

      like a stage when the doors opened the
curtains raised the hold of a slave ship

———————

               Comfortineachothersarms   dozingonhardbenches

———————

a monstrous monotonous droning
they swept on
south of the Borough by six o'clock the skies
empty Thameside blazed
as the sun began to sink the vast expanse
into the midst of a burning fiery furnace
of the red glow west and southwest a
chill to the heart

———————

Nicholson's gin factory in Poplar was hit
gin poured into the river Lea
one solid blue flame of burning gin
where it flows
under Bow Bridge

———————

Quebec Yard Surrey Docks the greater the cumulative heat the
fiercer the draught of cold air dragged in to feed
it the quicker the movement of the fire and the
greater the length of its flames they were so long
and their heat so great as to blister the paint
on fireboats tried to slip past under the lee of

the opposite river bank 300 yards away solid embers a
foot long tossed into streets to start fresh fires timber
the firemen had drenched began at once to steam then
dry then burst into flame in the intense heat radiated
pepper fires stinging particles burning when the firemen breathe rum
fires torrents of blazing liquid pouring from warehouse doors barrels

exploding like bombs paint fires another cascade of white-hot
flame coating the pumps with varnish could not be
cleaned for weeks rubber fires black clouds of choking smoke
sugar burning liquid floats on the water in dockland basins
tea blazes firemen pouring cold water on hot tea leaves
a plague of black flies around a bombed jam factory

———————

great orange walls of flame
as a timber dump took fire
across the Temple Mills Sidings

thousands tiny red
embers drift in the black

fires far to the north beyond Hampstead fires beyond West Ham stretching almost to Romford fires six miles to the west in Hammersmith fires eight miles south at Norwood and in the miles between never till now did I go through a tempest dropping fire

2200 fires out of control before midnight

railway lines blasted roads cratered 700 gas mains fractured across the City water mains destroyed a two-acre waste-paper dump Farmiloe's Paint Works in Battersea 250,000 books at the British Museum Fields' Candle Factory 6,000,000 Red Cross flags and 10,000 collecting tins Beckton Gas Works blown sky-high

Lambeth Palace McDougall's flour mills cable and wireless headquarters in Moorgate unsold copies of *Murphy* the Royal College of Surgeons the skeletons of kangaroos brought back by Captain Cook six acres of rubber and anchovy sauce at Hammersmith the sixteenth-century hall of Gray's Inn a mound of ash

10,000 pairs of shoes in Freeman, Hardy and Willis Salvation Army Headquarters bonded brandy and cigars at Waterloo Station £100,000 worth of Gordon's gin in the City Road House of Commons the roof of the 350-foot Victoria Tower blazed the roof of the Abbey fell in with a roar

———————

enormous uprush of white light a gigantic mushroom with a huge black cap and for a moment square miles brilliantly illuminated direct hit on the largest gas-holder in the gas-works off Purley Way

five million cubic feet of gas
burned off in a few seconds

——————

Docks ablaze after the sun sets
inside the Cathedral light
I have never seen the stained-glass windows
glow as they did then
western skies already dark

fierce red glow a burning fiery furnace in the East struck fast for the first time
that black London roof-scape silhouette   copper-orange sky

——————

a flock of pigeons circling around
overhead all night they seemed
lost as if they couldn't understand
the unnatural dawn all night it
looked like sunrise

around us the pigeons
white in the glare birds of peace

———————

St Giles Cripplegate the bomb blew a hole in the north-west wall

the statue of Milton outside was knocked off its pedestal almost undamaged Milton's bust inside was untouched

———————

darkened street the sky aglow
searchlights and stars of bursting

shells over East London from
Paddington Street searchlights and parachute

flares every building floodlit white
glare of parachute flares tracers

the sky lit up gun-flashes
sheet-lightning background of stars

———————

under the old copper roofing of the British Museum incendiaries burning fiercely in the high rafters choking black smoke

not only the rafters burning but the Roman Britain Room the Prehistoric Room the Greek Bronze Room empty now of treasures

suddenly a roar the flames wrapped around the southwest quadrant book-stack climbing into the sky a tempest dropping fire

───────────

two sticks of bombs had blasted forty houses
killing 11 people outright injuring
70 survivors swarmed through the streets
bare feet
over broken glass through
pools of blazing varnish

───────────

Near the Elephant and Castle a pub
open a roaring trade
4 in the morning

"Drink the beer while it's here"

light of the fires a fiery furnace

red on the swinging pub sign
THE WORLD'S END

———————

narrow crossroads near Fleet Street one corner block
was well alight walls fallen away doors and windows floors
inside alight and dropping the other only half gone but
fire was eating it up a glow appeared in
its dark windows panes cracked flames gushed out and
soon that too was laid open a boom and a
roar the gas main went a girder became red-hot
and sagged a piece of crumpled metal a foot square
fell on the pavement and slowly uncurled the whole alleyway
covered with smoke a blizzard of red-hot snow

———————

Her father: 'They say they are having another evacuation. Now will you go?'
'No I want to stay here.'
'You've just seen. You want to be safe don't you?'
(Sobbing): 'I want to stay here, with you.'

———————

January 11th a bomb caused the road to the
station suddenly dark the moment collapse into
Bank Station subway the escalators people
crushed

or blasted to death a train was entering
blast travelled down demolished the bomb fell
the death-roll was one hundred and eleven

———————

a ticking time-bomb
carried away in the boot of a taxi

exploding
as it stood at traffic lights

———————

Tins of toffees dropped by enemy aeroplanes
shaped like handbags
a coloured tartan design
puzzle on the lid
Lyons Assorted Toffee and *Skotch*
to be handed immediately to the police
stating where found
with time and date

———————

"To the Editor of the Times – Sir, After the terrific bombing of London on Sunday night it speaks well for that city's organization and recovery powers that a letter posted right in the heart of the bombed area at 2.45pm on the following Monday was received at Weybridge at 7.20 on Tuesday morning."

[*The Times*: 2 Jan 1941]

———————

"The future is announced"

for Robert Sheppard

one flaming mass a burning fiery furnace a remarkable thing
anybody could get out of that area and when we saw people
the movement of people in the intervals of a storm
come streaming down from dockland we were absolutely amazed
women and children an army marching running
dirty and dishevelled streaming away from
danger carrying bundles over their shoulders hurrying to get away the
afternoon the docks were on fire people going past our house
like refugees just bundles turned out of their places nowhere to
go then all of a sudden the most horrible roar the

place got hit there was miles of us buried there the
A.R.P. trying to dig us out and transfer us to stretchers

in the road I'm afraid I don't remember much more I
was unconscious bodies on the footway in the road I stood
and watched for a few moments and eventually some of them
stood up to my relief they were not all dead but
some were stick after stick of bombs dropping into the flames
hurling burning wood embers showers of sparks hundreds of feet into

the air gangs of A.R.P. clearing earth from buried Anderson shelters and
bringing occupants dazed and half-suffocated out into the air heavy with
smoke and charred timber crockery pots and pans a few articles
of furniture pony carts barrows prams and cycles homeless shocked penniless
out of the borough destitute a steady stream at the Tube
Station almost every bus stop families with suitcases and packages making
their way out of danger many of them no longer had
a home and all they carried was the clothes they stood

_____

I heard something whistle and dropped we smelt carbide and suspected a calcium carbide incendiary

he came over again and we dropped in a flower bed behind a low wall guns flashed all around
about thirty yards away the low clouds threw back the flashes and overhead the plane droned and
periodically dropped his packet in the middle I remarked

it reminds you of the war films what price glory not a bit of it came the reply they had shell-holes to be in not rose bushes

————————

Down to Surrey Docks through flames
meeting from each side of the road
sparks and fragments
falling they beat off their trousers
and stamped out the ropes
and came back another way
past a wall that collapsed behind them

————————

Three soldiers going down Throgmorton Street uniforms topped by
top hats one carried an old umbrella they raised
their hats to the girls
and distributed paid cheques to admirers

————————

our wardens in Poplar a
very rough-and-ready crowd indeed
citizens of their own borough if they
liked you they probably called you
"mate" irrespective of your rank

if they thought you were just
passable they'd call you "mister"
and if they disliked you
they usually called you "sir"

———————

They was dropping different things all over London again I heard something come down and go with a dull thud it may have gone in the river I don't know then I heard a scraping metallic sound coming closer in the darkness I didn't stop to look I just took to my heels up Church Street as far and as fast as I could this noise was following rattling and scraping along the street and gaining I just belted hell for leather up the road I thought this darned thing whatever it is it can't turn round a corner surely so when I got to Paultons Street I turned the corner and this thing went by me it stopped up the road about a hundred yards further on in the half-light a dome-shaped object in the centre of the road I found this bloody dustbin lid chased me up the road

———————

In Leytonstone
Police Constable Horace Rutter
jumping from a tottering building
a six-year-old boy in his arms he
landed heavily
on a four-inch nail which
drove clean through his foot

———————

Buried 26 feet from the Cathedral wall in Dean's Yard a ton in weight

a vast hog above eight feet long and fitted with fuses

slipping further and further down 28 feet into the black mud under St Paul's

perilous toil a gas main burning nearby

after 3 days it was hauled out by two lorries in tandem

the streets were cleared and it was driven at high speed from St Paul's to Hackney Marshes

and left a 100-foot crater wide

———————

I went up on the roof with some of the firemen
to look at the City I've always remembered how I was
choked I think I was crying a little I could see

St. Paul's standing there and the fire all around and
I just said please God don't let it go I couldn't
help it I felt that if St. Paul's had gone something

would have gone from us but it stood in defiance it
did and when the boys were coming back the firemen said
it's bad but oh the old church stood it lovely that was

———————

       sometimes pumps kept everything at intervals
       hiss and crackle   noise of bombers

       flames and sometimes
       as if all blowing about
       film under a glass of dust
       stones and broken
       flames like skirts of
       fire but the noise was engines
       of the pumps and water throbbing

because

because all through that
week no one who was there
had any reason to suppose
that they and their city
would not be bombed and burned out of existence

———————

Old D– was nearly in tears over St Bride's I told him

better all the churches than a store full of grub he

just giggles at warehouse fires his teeth

wobbling like castanets the silly old bugger

———————

somebody called out there's another one coming
it wasn't a mine it was a man on the end of his
parachute and he dropped down fast over the
road and down on to the foreshore of the river

early twenties in a green flying suit and pretty
well the same colour himself he was very correct
in his behaviour didn't say anything didn't do
anything just stood more or less at attention

someone went down the steps along the embankment and got hold of a youngster in his out of the pocket on the leg of his flying suit I don't know what he'd have done if we hadn't wrested it from him and shortly afterwards two then somebody rushed up and kicked him in the seat very hard and succeeded in getting a pistol policemen marched the German airman off along the embankment   just as if he'd been drunk and disorderly on a Saturday night

––––––––––

Hoses not in ones and

twos but in dozens all

over the street in cold

dawn fires and smoulder drenched

to the skin a fine

spray like Irish rain grimy

firemen swayed eyes blood-red from

sparks play hoses on buildings

––––––––––

           embers falling like rain

      clattering on your helmet. Cheapside a mass of flames,

leaping from one side of the road to the other.

———————

Suspended by his heels from a crane a doctor
is lowered to the bottom of a hole
where a man is trapped
beside burning woodwork his head
only visible in the debris of his house
and injected morphia in his neck twice

———————

        Silence broken

        mobile generators
        feeding the lights the
        snow iron hard

sharp ring of picks and shovels

pools of glass under a black sky half

an acre of devastation

—————————

After noon it
stopped snowing

slithering in the slush

whole families standing
beside the remains of
their possessions

shivering waiting

case the looters moved in

doors windows ceilings all

gone the architecture of the world

—————————

A pear a red apple
inky black grapes and fat
plums emerald green leaves all
done in wax on
an ebonised stand covered with black
velvet protected from the world's
dust by a glass dome
bordered with red plush at
the centre of the mantelpiece
any more

———————

Muriel's house was
bombed her husband
standing among the
rooms ruins
just staring
unable to take himself away

———————

Well we have one little girl here he says not identified
and when I looked I'd never seen such a shock in
all my life all her little hair was burned and her

face where she'd put her fingers right across all the fire
was there well I suppose the Lord's taken her to be
right out of pain altogether I'd sooner her go that way

than be maimed for life a little cripple and then I
thought what about my mother and we never did find anything
of mother at all and I don't think a day goes

by without we don't talk of my mother and my little
daughter it was the Lord's way to take her and not
be injured and I still think we've got her with us

———————

don't know if I care much a
bomb's blown the outside of
my house down and my son
was killed three weeks ago at
New Malden he was coming

home from work and got to
the station the bomb dropped
on the booking office there
was nothing left of him
proper burial and a coffin but

what was in it nobody knows
I'm sure it wasn't my son now
my house has gone I don't
know

———————

One little boy of four

re-experiences the bomb

falling on the place his father

worked works

uneaten meal on the table

search for the lost body

endless inquiries at offices

waiting at the mortuary

every falling bomb is the bomb

killing his father

———————

of red-brick streets
Stoke Newington
scattering
granite across acres
and fragments of
corpses already dead two
land mines hit

———————

        buried for hours
and we could hear her
swearing away down there

can't think
where she learned the words
nice little old lady like that

———————

dust and chaos
marked the spot

'More open than usual'   John Lewis

dangerous tottering frame
of building London's

deserted cold winds
whistling empty screens
of damaged stone

———————

Portland Place Broadcasting House
a bomb crashed through the News Room

fourth and fifth floors gone
lower floors awash in a sea of paper in the dim light
from the illuminated
"Exit" notices

————————

asphalt platforms steam like coffee cooling

great sweep of Regent Street deserted

everyone except police and salvage workers

thoroughfare in a dead city. It would have been no surprise to see grass growing up out of the pavements

covered instead with a fine frosty glitter of powdered glass

————————

windows blown tumbled wreckage of
rubble in the road.

Front cut away – a doll's house
parlour where the evening meal was being eaten at the cloth-covered table, a teapot
and a bowl of tomatoes. Pictures knocked crooked by the blast

high in the air the useless bath and lavatory little
roll of toilet paper affixed to the door
staircase to an upper floor no longer exists

_____

random encounters most nights of the month a black
nothingness   move your feet gingerly

fear

sound of passing feet hurrying footsteps early morning
after the 'All Clear' hurrying home

_____

Athenaeum liveried staff sweeping away debris disconcerted

Bishops step delicately as cats over litter

of broken glass everywhere the sound of

broken glass being swept off the streets

_____

In the wrecked Christie's building in King Street St. James
the fire-twisted steel bars of the main strong room
were cut through yesterday
     and the safe containing thousands of pounds of jewels
          in 144 lots
was blasted open

———————

      tram driver
      tears
      streaming down his face
      repeating over and over

      "My conductor's dead…
      He's dead, my conductor…"

———————

Ain't no place for women
but they don't like to be away from home
and they come back

corner of Smithy and Exmouth Street

many of them homeless

one about 35 crying and trying not to

a few clothes over her arm

Everything I have is gone

not that I mind I'm alive and that's all that matters

my husband's a fine one he kept scoffing at me for running into the street shelters

he said fancy running out like that stay indoors

but I wouldn't listen to him

good job too else where would I be now

he's looking for his shirt he won't look for my dresses no it's his shirt worries him

everything I ever worked for it took me

15 years to build it up and look at it now

nothing left

one child crying endlessly at the sight of the gaping windows

———————

Monotony

Rationing

Queues

Girls in Air Force Blue
Need Oda-Ro-No

And shrouds
Counted and identified

Vaseline on eyelids for the dewy look

Damaged retinas

Compound fractures

Mouth full of brick-dust

Auxiliary Red

———————

shows advertising themselves as "strip teases"
claiming to present the naked female form on stage. The Lord Chamberlain
has threatened to withdraw licences from any premises
which offend against decency
and decorum.

———————

first sirens sounding the All Clear in the
distance the sirens under Albert Bridge it was
five to five the ordinary cold quiet of

early morning through smoke and a rain of charred
paper the sun was coming up people crunched
on rubble and broken glass shovelling human remains

into bins around the corner at the Cross
Keys one wall blown into the Bar
serving spirits hard as they could go

———————

In the streets debris of   stanchions and cast-iron   broken bricks if crushed and
broken bricks joists beams   columns can be used for   mixed with sand makes
and rafters doors window-   repairs beams making   aggregate for concrete to fill
frames steel girders   punchions and shoring   bomb craters in the road

———————

He smashed up me home and me missus in the same night

I just went down the Post   and when I come back it was flat as   as this here wharfside

there was just my house like   well   part of my house

missus were making me a cup of tea   for when I come home   she were in the passage between the kitchen and the wash-house where it blowed her

she were burnt right up to her waist   her legs were just two cinders …   and her face … the only thing I could recognize her by was one of her boots

I'd have lost fifteen homes if I could have kept my missus   we used to read together   I can't read meself she used to read to me like   we'd have our arm chairs one either side of the fire and she read me bits of the paper

we had a paper every evening every evening

—————

Three ragged blackened walls
a scroll on some yellow plaster
and a warped stained glass window

all that remains of St Mildred's Bread Street

—————

Commons debating chamber
steel girders charred timbers and masses of masonry
cover the green benches the Speaker's Chair the table of the house the two brass-bound despatch boxes

the upper part of the west wall has collapsed into Star Chamber Court littered with blocks of stone statues buried under debris in the lobby

———————

"I marvelled at the freaks of air raid damage and the unfathomable laws of blast. Scattered cherubs' wings and stone roses were strewn about – whole memorial plaques of carved marble had been blown across the width of the church and lay undamaged. The entire frontage of the deserted business opposite was wrecked, and Milton's statue had been flung from its plinth. Yet the lamp-post was standing erect with no pain of its lantern broken."

[Cecil Beaton, *The Years Between. Diaries, 1939-44* (New York, 1965), p.37.]

———————

The property market during 1940 showed a diminution of business
sales of all classes of country properties proceeded more steadily

mainly business houses anxious to preserve their records and accommodate
staff where work could be carried on with the least

interruption the private buyer has come to the fore in
the past few months following London's heavy bombing higher prices

have resulted and demand still grows great difficulty is now
experienced in finding suitable houses in so-called safe areas property

in 'less safe' areas offers tempting opportunities to the speculative
buyer and with the Government's War Damage Compensation Bill a

greater volume of business should result

———————

'the plump and confident boy at the end of the row'

Ribbentrop's son
in a photograph

Athletics Team 1937

picked up from a slush of black watery slime in
the burnt-out charred and roofless wreck
of Westminster School 15 May 1941

———————

smoke charred papers embers

drifting over fields and woods
30 miles away

a grave in the air

———————

a rescue party had uncovered
the head and shoulders of a child
buried standing up and dead

rain was pelting down and
I can see now that
child's head and shoulders above

the debris white-faced and
clean where the rain had
splashed and washed his face

———————

When it ended nobody knew
it was over all the time

I was evacuated I told myself one day
all this will be over and I can go

home again where I used to live everything was
obliterated I couldn't find where my house was

more than fifty years ago I'm still waiting to go home again

———————

St Christopher's without number

poppies and buttercups

among mounds of yellow rubble

urchins with shrapnel to sell

whooped through the ruins

———————

Note

This is not a work of history, in any recognisable sense anyway. In these pages I have appropriated, spliced, edited and rewritten testimony from sources such as contemporary newspapers and magazines, memoirs, oral histories, documentary films and so on – too many to list here. And I have reassembled them in various forms.

Instead of a commentary or a rationale let me offer these questions posed by Foucault:

"We would no longer hear the questions that have been rehashed for so long: Who really spoke? Is it really he and not someone else? With what authenticity or originality? And what part of his deepest self did he express in his discourse? Instead, there would be other questions, like these: What are the modes of existence of this discourse? Where has it been used, how can it circulate, and who can appropriate it for himself? What are the places in it where there is room for possible subjects? Who can assume these various subject functions? And behind all these questions, we would hear hardly anything but the stirring of an indifference: What difference does it make who is speaking?"
 — Michel Foucault, 'What Is an Author?' in *Essential Works of Foucault,* Vol. 2: *Aesthetics, Method, and Epistemology,* edited by James D. Faubion, translated by Robert Hurley and others (New York: The New Press, 1999), p.222.

But anybody who wants further reflection on method might look up the 'Postface' to John Seed, *Brandon Pithouse: Recollections of the Durham Coalfield* (Middlesborough: Smokestack Books, 2016).

I should mention a few printed sources that have been particularly interesting and which a reader might want to follow up:

The Illustrated London News (1940-1941).

The Protection of Your Home Against Air Raids (London: Home Office 1938).

The Blitz (Mass Observation Teaching Booklet No.1: Mass Observation Archive, University of Sussex, 1987).

Amy Helen Bell, *London Was Ours. Diaries and Memoirs of the London Blitz* (London: Tauris 2008).

Stephen Bungay, *The Most Dangerous Enemy: A History of the Battle of Britain* (London: Aurum Press 2001).

Angus Calder, *The Myth of the Blitz* (London: Pimlico 1991).

Olivia Cockett, *Love and War in London. A Woman's Diary 1939-1942*, edited by Robert Malcolmson (Waterloo, ONT.: Wilfred Laurier University Press 2005).

Richard Collier, *The City That Would Not Die. The Bombing of London, May 10-11, 1941* (New York: Dutton 1960).

Geoffrey Fields, 'Nights Underground in Darkest London. The Blitz, 1940-1941' *Cercles* 17, 181-217.

Constantine Fitzgibbon, *The Winter of the Bombs. The Story of the Blitz of London* (New York: Norton 1957).

Anna Freud and Dorothy Burlingham, *War and Children* (London: Medical War Books 1943).

James Hinton, *Nine Wartime Lives. Mass-Observation and the Making of the Modern Self* (Oxford: Oxford University Press 2010)

Ralph Ingersoll, *Report on England. November 1940* (New York: Simon and Schuster 1940).

Robert Mackay, *Half the Battle. Civilian morale in Britain during the Second World War* (Manchester: Manchester University Press 2002).

Kristine A. Miller, *British Literature of the Blitz. Fighting the People's War* (Basingstoke: Palgrave 2009).

John Ray, *The Night Blitz, 1940-1941* (London: Cassell 1996)

Philip Ziegler, *London at War 1939-1945* (London: Sinclair-Stevenson 1995)

Lightning Source UK Ltd.
Milton Keynes UK
UKOW07f1517070815

256544UK00002B/18/P

9 781848 614321